GATEWAY TO SURVIVAL
IS STORAGE

GATEWAY TO SURVIVAL IS STORAGE

—by Walter D. Batchelor

Published by

HAWKES PUBLISHING INC.
156 W. 2170 S. (Box 15711)
Salt Lake City, Utah 84115
Please phone: (801) 487-1695
or Toll Free: (800) 453-4616

Copyright, 1974, by
WALTER D. BATCHELOR

Printed in the U.S.A.

First Printing 1937
Fourteenth Printing 1974

International Standard Book No. 0-88290-027-7

Printing—Typesetting—Binding
by
HAWKES PUBLISHING INC.

ACKNOWLEDGMENT

The author thanks all who have contributed information and suggestions in order to make this publication possible.

PREFACE

Back in the late 1930's the meager amount of storage data, then available, was assembled and published by the author. In the early 1950's additional information was compiled and the Second Edition was published in booklet form. The Third Edition, published in May 1961, received wide acclaim nationally from Civil Defense and the food processing industry because of its complete, easy-to-understand storage guidance. Subsequent editions have been distributed throughout the world and permission was granted in the early 1970's to translate the booklet into German, Spanish, and French. Total printing is approaching a quarter-million copies.*

This LATEST EDITION has been extensively revised and updated, contains the latest ideas about the storage of food and other products, and presents a practical, effective approach to the solution of storage problems. Workable, time-tested plans are outlined step-by-step. Now, every serious-minded family can respond intelligently to this sober admonition: "Prepare yourselves for possible emergencies, against hard times, inflation and scarcity, by maintaining a year's reserve of items that will keep you alive; food, clothing, fuel for warmth, cooking and light, basic medical supplies, seeds for gardens, and items for cleanliness.

A successful storage program can be achieved without difficulty if a person will take to carefully **study** this booklet and then apply its simple storage rules. Most important of all, one should become thoroughly familiar with the ways to preserve various foods in order to maintain their nutrition. Remember, success comes to those who "learn to do by doing."

TABLE OF CONTENTS

Section I   Planning Ahead 13
Section II   Developing the Plan 17
Section III   What Should We Store................. 21
Section IV   Storing to Prevent Spoilage 27
Section V   Notes on Specific Foods 31
               Fruits and Vegetables 31
               Canned Fruit Juice................ 31
               Canned Milk (evaporated) 32
               Fats and Oils..................... 32
               Canned Meat and Meat
               Products 34
               Cheese 34
               Home-Canned Fish 34
               Wheat and Other Grains 36
               Flour 39
               Rice, Beans, Peas and TVP........ 39
               Introduction to TVP 40
               Dried Milk (nonfat)............... 43
               Dried and Dehydrated Fruits and
               Vegetables 44
               Eggs 45
               Sugar 46
               Honey 46
               Cereals, Prepared Breakfast
               Foods, Macaroni, etc. 46

	Salt............................. 47
	Baking Powder and Soda 47
	Dry Yeast....................... 47
	Water.......................... 48
Section VI	Food Dehydrating in the Home........ 53
Section VII	Rotate Your Perishables 65
Section VIII	Homemade Products................. 73
Section IX	What About Civil Defense? 77
	Survival Kit..................... 80
	Medical Supplies (memo list) 82
Section X	Emergency Sanitation 85
Section XI	Nutritional Table.................... 91
Section XII	Medical Supplies 95
Section XIII	Memo List of Storage Items.......... 99
Section XIV	Notes on Fumigation and Temperature 103

SEC. I

PLANNING AHEAD

SECTION I

PLANNING AHEAD

Rare indeed are the undertakings that succeed without a plan and a purpose.

Successful storage does not come by chance, nor without effort. Success comes to those who are willing to spend some thought in planning it—and then carrying out the plan. A half-hearted effort in any storage program usually results in great waste and expense. Spoilage is bound to occur with consequent waste of food and money.

"The Lord looks with disfavor upon waste. He has blessed His people with abundant crops. The Lord is doing His part, and He expects us to do ours." (Conference Report, April 1942.)

The most important storage rules are found on page 18. These rules should be **studied** and made a part of **every** storage plan. It is a proven fact, by long experience, that failure to observe **all** of the three storage rules will end in outright failure or inadequate storage. **Example:** During the 1967-68 Kennecott Copper Company strike in Utah, one of the employees said, "I completely used up my year's supply of food in six weeks."

No one questions the wisdom of having sufficient food and supplies stored to supply a family throughout an emergency. Depression, accident, illness, loss of job, strikes, earthquakes, wars, floods, or death of the breadwinner are merely a few of the disasters that could affect a family. Due to our very complex society most of us depend directly upon others to sustain our lives. Widespread disaster in areas far away from our community could have serious effect upon our daily lives. For example, a sudden influx into our community of displaced persons from danger areas considerable distances away would quickly exhaust available supplies from our stores and markets. Transportation systems could easily become clogged. Profiteers would undoubtedly prey upon the public and those supplies that were available would sky-rocket in price beyond our means.

Anyone can guess what might happen. We frankly do not know how soon or what event might occur which would require us to live from our storage, but we do know that a wise person will heed the counsel to store for a year ahead.

SEC. II

DEVELOPING
THE PLAN

SECTION II

DEVELOPING THE PLAN

A plan to suit the needs of **your** family then becomes our first consideration. What others are storing for their families may not be at all suitable for you. There is no such thing as one best storage plan. Appetites of families and individuals are not the same, storage conditions vary greatly in different parts of the world, general storage instructions could not possibly apply to all people living in many climates...these are some of the reasons no one should tell you specifically what to store. So here is the first guideline in developing your plans:

RULE 1.

It is most important that you store **only** those items your family will use.

However, if you have the space, we urge you to store additional permanent foods or household supplies (see page 34) to be used for barter.

Much food is wasted through spoilage or changes in appetites because it is stored too long or in quantities too large for normal consumption habits of your family and purchase **no more** than will be used within the period covered by your storage program. Numerous persons have purchased in case lots, thinking that it was more economical to save a few cents on each case, only to end up by throwing away a portion of the case due to spoilage and thereby wasting many dollars. Consequently, you **must** keep all **moisture-packed** (wet) foods

in rotation within a two-year period (or less) due to the spoilage potential and to prevent loss of essential vitamins and nutrients. Other than a few permanent-type foods listed in Section V, which will store for longer periods, it is best to:

RULE 2.

Purchase perishables in quantities **no larger** than the normal requirements of your family within your planned rotation period (two years or less).

CAUTION: After two years' storage, **most** perishable foods (canned or bottled in moisture) will rapidly lose their food value, due to dissipation of vitamins, so do not store them longer than **two** years.

RULE 3.

You cannot keep a year's supply **on hand**, nor successfully store canned or bottled foods without spoilage, unless you faithfully follow a rotation plan. (See Section VII, page 65.)

IMPORTANT: Don't be mislead into group buying projects, such as "item of the month," bulk purchases, or case lots, **unless** the items you buy fit the above three (3) rules.

SEC. III

WHAT SHOULD WE STORE?

SECTION III

WHAT SHOULD WE STORE?

Three suggested plans are given below for your guidance. The plans can be used as given or altered to suit your needs and storage conditions. If you alter these plans, it would be wise to refer to the Nutritional Table in Section XI to make sure that you maintain the essential protein in your diet.

One item in particular should be in EVERY plan—vitamin C tablets. From 45-50 mg. (milligrams) per day is needed for each person because this vitamin will not store in the body, so you need a renewed supply every day in order to maintain good health.

PLAN 1.

You should initially determine your storage requirements by sitting down with your family and making a list of foods and household necessities you **know** you use. If this is done, each member of your family will be recognized and, having participated, will tend to increase his interest in the storage plan. (The list thus developed will be used as a work sheet and permanent reference hereafter, so keep it on heavy bond or ledger paper so as to preserve it). Write the list on the left side of the paper. Make 13 vertical columns to the right of the list, with each column headed by a month plus a TOTAL for the year. Next plot the quantities you **know** you will use of each item under each month. If you cannot easily determine this, you should make an accurate record of

every item consumed in your home over a three (3) month period—canned and permanent foods, household supplies, medical items, etc.—and your year's requirement plotted from this record. Your worksheet will then look something like this:

	JAN	FEB	MAR	APR	MAY	JUNE	JULY	AUG	SEPT	OCT	NOV	DEC	1 YR. TOTAL
CANNED FOODS													
Corn, whole kernel	2	2	2	2	2	2	1	0	0	0	1	2	16
Tuna fish	5	6	5	6	5	6	2	0	0	3	5	6	49
Soup, chicken nood.	8	8	8	6	4	3	2	2	2	3	6	8	60
etc., etc.,													
DEHYDRATED FOODS													
Potatoes, No. 10 can	1	1	1	1	1	1	1	1	1	1	1	1	12
etc., etc.,						(list other quantities)							
PERMANENT FOODS													
Wheat, lbs.	100	100	100	0	100	0	100	0	100	0	100	100	800
ect., etc.						(list other quantities)							
HOUSEHOLD SUPPLIES													
* * * *						etc., etc.							
MEDICAL SUPPLIES													
* * * *						etc., etc.							

After completing your worksheets, it is our recommendation that you purchase the absolute necessities first, such as those listed in PLAN 2 below. These are "existence" supplies which we urge you to get **now** so you will at least have survival amounts on hand while you are building up your storehouse of other products.

Purchase the quantities indicated in the "TOTAL" column if your storage plan is for one year. See Section VI herein for a successful rotation plan for perishable products.

PLAN 2.

Of course, many individuals will want to store only sufficient quantities for an "existence" diet. Others may have different ideas as to what the basic foods are, but from research we have conducted, we recommend the following quantities for an existence diet. Also shown is the period of time the products will keep without spoiling. How to store these items is explained in Section V. (The word "indefinite" means no limit.)

Product	Average Adult Requirement/year	Storage Period
Wheat, whole kernel, hard	185 lbs.*	Indefinite
Milk, dry nonfat, powdered (365 qts.)	75 lbs.	Varies***
Sugar, granulated	20 lbs.	Indefinite
Honey, pure, unadulterated	24 lbs.	Indefinite
Shortening, canned, or vegetable oil**	12 lbs.	2 years
Peas, dried split	18 lbs.	Indefinite
Beans, dried, plus miscellaneous hermetically packed dehydrated vegetables (if you use them)	60 lbs. (beans)	Indefinite
Raisins, plus miscellaneous hermetically packed dehydrated fruits (if you use them)	24 lbs. raisins	2 years for raisins
Vitamin C tablets, 50 mg (store in the dark)	365	5 years
Vitamin tablets, 1-A-Day type	365	2 years
Salt, iodized	2 lbs.	Indefinite
Baking powder (for average amount of baking)	1 lb.	2 years
Baking Soda	1 pkg.	Indefinite
Live dry yeast (you need this to make "everlasting yeast," explained in Section VII)	3 pkgs. or	Expiration on
Grinder (for flour and cracked cereal)	1 vac. can	package, or 6 months at 70°

Don't Forget Essential Household and Medical Supplies. (See Section XII)

* If circumstances cause wheat to become the principal diet, the amount required per individual is somewhat greater.

** Some oils, such as Wesson, may keep many years.

*** See Section V – Dried Milk (nonfat).

PLAN 3.

Rural and farm houses are quite often better equipped to store foods safely for a longer period than city homes. For those who have the proper storage facilities such as root cellars for fresh fruits and vegetables, and other fresh farm products, we list the

following items which are based on average adult requirements. Some family members will need more of
some foods, less of others. Small children usually need
smaller servings, while adolescent boys and girls need
much larger portions to meet their requirements. You
should adjust these amounts then according to the age
group of your family, the types of work in which they are
engaged, and their physical condition.

Product	Average Adult Requirement/Year
Milk	365 qts.
Eggs	30 doz.
Meat	150 lbs.
Vegetables and Fruits:	
Green and yellow colored	170 lbs.
Carrots and cabbage	35 lbs.
Potatoes	150 lbs.
Tomatoes and citrus fruits	120 lbs.
Other fruits and vegetables	200 lbs.
Apples	75 lbs.
Flour, cereals, bread (or whole kernel wheat)	185 lbs.
Dried beans, split peas, nuts	85 lbs.
Fats and Oils:	
Butter, cream, shortening, bacon, salad oils	65 lbs.
Sugar, syrup, honey, preserves, jelly, candy	60 lbs.

SPECIAL NOTE:

There are two types of storage programs: 1)perma-
nent or indefinite-type items, and 2) rotated or
perishable-types. It is recommended that the
permanent-type items be procured first. These are paper
products, soaps, cleansers, etc.

A prominent grocer stated that 25-40% of the items
stocked in grocery stores were "eye appeal" and were un-
necessary in a family's food budget. Before completing
your storage plans, then, you should consider storing
only the basic nutritional foods and the household
necessities of your family—and eliminate the un-
necessary 25-40%.

SEC. IV

STORING TO
PREVENT SPOILAGE

SECTION IV

STORING TO PREVENT SPOILAGE

An ideal storage room for preserved food is a cool room in the basement that is dry all seasons of the year, free from steam, hot water and hot air pipes, odors (kerosene, onions, soap, petroleum products) and closed off from the rest of the house. Under these conditions the yearly temperature would be between 50 and 60 degrees F. The door to this room should be opened only to remove food items. Exposures of cool canned goods to warm, moist air will cause rusting of the cans. Food in rusted cans is good if there has been no perforation in the wall of the can. If a basement room is not available, a closet or garage on the north side of the house may be used. It should be remembered that in peace or war, whenever disaster strikes, canned foods are the safest form of foods.

Ideal storage temperature for canned, bottled, and packaged goods is 40 degrees F. in a dry place, the darker the better. **Do not allow canned or bottled foods containing liquid to freeze.** The ice would break the jars and may break the seal on both glass jars and tin cans.

Store nothing on cement flooring. Place slats of lumber between cement and storage to prevent sweating or rusting.

A few vitamins may be damaged by heat. The cold-pack process of canning, according to the directions of a good manual, causes the least heat and oxidation damage to foods. One or two vitamins are damaged by light, so **keep bottled foods in the dark** if possible. Cartons the bottles were purchased in is an excellent protection from light.

Quick-freezing is an excellent method for retaining both flavor and nutritive values of many types of fresh foods. Dehydrated foods also retain these qualities. There is certainly no objection to home freezers, but don't forget the possible electric power failures.

Home or factory canned products which are bulged (full of fermentation gas) should be destroyed. Home canned or bottled beans, corn, and meat ought to be heated in an open pan after opening, heated at boiling temperatures for 20 minutes.

Canned goods, purchased from the markets, should be stored **no longer than two years.** After that time, the product may still be good to eat, but it may not be as palatable nor contain the essential nutrients for good health as the fresher products. Therefore, home and factory canned and bottled **goods must be rotated.** See Section VII, page 65.

SEC. V

NOTES ON
SPECIFIC FOODS

SECTION V

NOTES ON SPECIFIC FOODS

A. CANNED AND BOTTLED FOODS

Fruits and Vegetables

Only high quality canned goods and vegetables should be stored. Avoid the "bargain sales" of canned goods where the canner or store owner may unload inferior merchandise or old stock. There are several local as well as many nationally known labels of good quality. It is also better to purchase your storage goods from a store or market that has a rapid turnover of goods to insure that you are buying fresher merchandise.

These canned goods should be stored in cool, dry places between 35 and 60 degrees F. Never store foods in the furnace room or near steam, hot water or hot air pipes. If the food is in glass containers, it should be stored in the dark. Most canned goods stored in the above temperature range can be kept for two years with only slight losses in vitamins and changes in color, flavor, and texture. Fruits with pits, such as cherries and plums, should not be stored for more than a year. There is an appreciable loss of Thiamin and vitamin C, as well as flavor and color changes, in food stored above 80 degrees F.

Canned Fruit Juice (unfrozen)

With the exception of pineapple and tomato juice, fruit juices are rather unstable even under recommended storage conditions. They readily undergo marked changes in flavor and color. Cans of juice should not be allowed to stand on the shelf more than a year.

Canned Milk (evaporated)

If canned milk is stored at a temperature of 40 to 50 degrees F, it can be successfully kept for about a year. Do not figure on a longer storage period.

It is recommended that cans in storage be inverted (turned upside down) once every 60 days to prevent fat separation. High temperatures in storage will produce dark color, strong flavor, and in some cases fat separation in a very few months. A darker color develops as the storage period lengthens, but this is not necessarily a sign of spoilage. Give the can a few vigorous shakes before opening. If fat separation has occurred, the shaking will return the milk to a smooth solution that pours easily. This also prevents a watery and lumpy texture. One tall can of evaporated milk is equivalent to about 80% of one quart of fluid whole milk.

Fats and Oils

When shortenings and oils are purchased, the size of the container should be considered. Big quantities left open over extended periods of time should be avoided. Three-pound size cans of shortening (hydrogenated vegetable oil) and one-quart size bottles of oil would be ideal for a family consuming 12 to 18 pounds of shortening or oil per year. Oil should be rotated to avoid a storage period longer than one year, unless the storage period is known to be longer. Vegetable oil, for example, may keep many years. Pure vegetable shortening should be rotated within two years after purchase if kept at temperatures below 60 degrees F. Higher temperatures will bring on rancidity much quicker.

a. Butter

Good butter will keep well over a year when frozen. It's best if made from rich pasteurized sweet cream and is left unsalted.

b. Margarine

Although presently less expensive, margarines are as nutritious as butter. All brands are required to contain at least 15,000 units of vitamin A per pound (well above the average for butter). It's best to buy those brands of margarine also containing 1000 to 2000 units of vitamin D, in addition to A. Read the label.

Margarine will keep well over a year if stored in a home freezer. At ordinary refrigerator temperature, however, flavor deteriorates rapidly. Unless you have a home freezer, don't buy more than a few months' supply.

c. Lard

Commercial shortenings will keep longer than factory packaged or home-made lard. Even at home freezer temperatures the best rendered lard most likely will not keep longer than 6 to 8 months unless antioxidents are purchased from the drug store and mixed with the lard.

Rancid lard develops from poor rendering methods. When you try to render lard yourself, make sure all the water is evaporated. Don't drain off any of the lard until the cracklings are a deep golden brown. Put a lid on the kettle when you think the lard is about ready to pour off. Leave it on a few minutes, then look to see if any moisture has collected on the inside of the lid. As long as there is any moisture inside the lid, you still have water in the lard. It's best to keep lard under refrigeration.

Canned Meat and Meat Products

Canned meat, meat products, poultry, and fish have generally the same shelf life as fruits and vegetables when stored under conditions recommended above. Canned hams are, in general, perishable items and should be stored under refrigerated conditions unless the container indicates otherwise, such as on some small hams.

Cheese

Cheese will not mold if it is wrapped for freezing and kept frozen. Most cheeses will last two years in a frozen condition, while others should be rotated in about one year. Experience of your own with your favorite types will tell you the proper rotation period.

Home-Canned Fish

The rapid depletion of sea foods, particularly fish, in the Atlantic and Pacific Oceans bordering the United States is the result of overfishing the continental waters by foreign nations. Canned salmon, for example, has increased in cost to five times its price in just two short years. The fishing industry and the U.S. Government have become so alarmed at the near exhaustion of some fish species that legislation is being considered to deny foreign nations the right to fish within 200 miles of our coastlines.

It is recognized that many consumers include fish in their everyday diet, not only for economy but for weight-watching, special diets, and nutrition. So that we may be of help to those individuals who are able to either catch fresh fish or produce them at a reasonable price, we have developed a canning technique, described below. We feel that the taste of fish, canned in this method, will appeal to almost everyone:

RECIPE FOR ONE-HALF (½) PINT JARS

1. Thoroughly clean the fish, cut off the heads, fins, and tails. Remove the scales (if any) but **do not** skin or fillet the fish. The bones and skin will become soft during cooking, the same as with other canned fish.

2. Cut fish in 3½ inch lengths and pack vertically in the jars as tightly as possible **without forcing.**

3. Place on top of fish in the packed jar:

    One-half (½) teaspoon of table salt
    One-half (½) teaspoon of vinegar, white or brown
    One (1) tablespoon of pure olive oil.
    (No other oils will do...**do not substitute**)

4. Screw cap on jar, then loosen cap slightly in order to release the pressure buildup in the jar which occurs during cooking.

5. Place the filled jars in the pressure cooker, on the cooking rack, and **cover the rack** with water. Close the pressure cooker and set the pressure regulator to ten (10) pounds.

6. When the pressure reaches ten pounds, then cook the fish at a **constant ten-pound pressure** for one and one-half (1½) hours.

7. Turn off the heat and let the pressure return to zero

before removing the jars. Remove the jars and tighten the caps thoroughly.

8. Store the jars in a cool, dry place for **not over** two (2) years. It would be much more preferable to replace the canned fish **each year.**

If you prefer to can fish in PINTS, then double both the ingredients and the cooking time. We strongly urge you **not** to can in larger containers than pints.

B. DRIED AND DEHYDRATED FOODS

A proven and successful container for dried foods is a one-gallon bottle with wide mouth and screw lid. Bulk purchases of dried foods should be immediately placed in permanent containers, such as tightly sealed bottles or the metal containers described under **Wheat** below. To leave the food in the original burlap sack, plastic or paper bags would subject it to insect infestation and moisture condensation, both of which invite spoilage.

CAUTION: Some plastic containers give off an offensive odor that will penetrate the food stored therein and make it unfit to eat. So make sure the plastic container is approved for storing foodstuffs before you use it. Most of the **hard** plastic containers, glazed inside, are suitable for use.

Wheat and Other Grains

Many problems involved in the storage of wheat can be avoided if wheat is purchased from a reputable miller. He should be informed of your intention and asked to supply you with a clean, insect free, dry (less than 10% moisture) hi-protein wheat. If this wheat is properly stored, as described in the following paragraphs, it can be preserved indefinetely without undergoing deterioration.

Do not store **soft** wheat for food. Purchase dark, hard, winter wheat (turkey red) or dark, hard, spring or Marquis wheat. Protein should be above 11.50 per cent. The miller will know the protein content.

A good container for wheat is a metal, airtight, or five-gallon, square can and with at least a seven-inch diameter opening in the top with a friction lid. This container, as well as the one-gallon bottles described above, is a proper barrier to insects, rodents, moisture and air. Three five-gallon cans will store approximately 100 pounds of wheat. The cans of wheat should be stored under the same conditions of temperature and moisture as mentioned under canned goods above.

Unless it is treated, a **high** percentage of stored wheat is lost to infestation due to the presence of weevil eggs not evident at the time of purchase, so one of the following treatments is advised:

1. Crushed dry ice may be spread inside over the bottom of the container and the wheat immediately placed over the top of the dry ice. Each 100 pounds of wheat will require about 8 ounces of dry ice which, of course, should be crushed just before using to prevent evaporation. Sufficient time should be allowed for the dry ice to volatilize before placing the lid on the container (approximately 30 minutes). **WARNING:** Too much dry ice will develop pressure within the container and may cause it to explode. Therefore, should pressure develop (bulging), cautiously remove the lid momentarily to allow the pressure to escape and then replace the lid. This procedure should be repeated as necessary to release all excessive pressure, and should be carried out

in a rather dry atmosphere to minimize the condensation of moisture on the bottom of the can. Vapors of the dry ice will penetrate all parts of the container, killing the insects and larvae. However, the wheat weevil eggs, if present, are not harmed by these vapors. It is necessary, then, that the vapors are present in an **airtight** container should the eggs hatch out.

2. Experiments have been conducted by some of the Agricultural Colleges to determine other methods that may be used for insect control and the safe protection of grains. Following are two methods that have been recommended, but no information has been given as to their effect on sprouting. After treatment by either method, store the grain in containers with tight-fitting lids:

a. Grain which shows no signs of infestations may be placed in shallow pans and heated in an oven for one-half hour at 140° F. Be sure to prop the oven door open slightly to prevent scorching the grain as this will destroy some of the vital nutrients.

b. Thorough freezing will also destroy an infestation. Because many insect eggs are very resistant to destruction, the grain requires freezing for a minimum of ten (10) days at a temperature of minus 10° F. to minus 20° F.

Fumigation with other products, such as bay leaves, silica aerogels, diatomaceous earth, etc., should be **completely avoided** inasmuch as our long experience has proven these products to be unreliable as fumigants. For the protection of other WHOLE grains, see Section XIV. NO grain should be stored in temperatures above 83° due to the rancidity potential.

Grains that have been prepared for cereal, such as oat flakes, should be fumigated with dry ice because chloride mixtures and the like could penetrate the cereal and make it un'edible.

If wheat is ground for cereal or flour, it should be consumed within five (5) days to derive the greatest nutritional benefit. After grinding, oxidation of the vitamins in the wheat begins immediately and many of them will dissipate in a few days. For this reason, millers are required to "enrich" flour by synthetically replacing usually 4 to 6 of the more than 20 organic nutrients stored in the wheat kernel which are lost in milling. There are many excellent whole wheat recipes and cook books on the market that you should try using with your home-ground, whole wheat flour.

Flour

We do not recommend the storing of flour for three major reasons: 1) It has lost much of the organic nutrients found in the wheat kernel; 2) Flour is too dense (compacted) to be successfully fumigated; and 3) It is more difficult to store than whole grain wheat and may develop a smelly off-flavor after long storage. However, if you wish to store flour, only the amount of flour normally used in one year should be stored. It then should be used regularly and replaced with fresh flour as it is used. Off-flavor flour may be improved by sifting a few times to aerate it. Store in containers that will ward off outside attacks by insects and rodents, and be sure to keep it dry.

Rice, Beans, Peas and TVP (Textured Vegetable Protein)

Rice, dried beans (pinto, navy, lima, pink, chili, etc.) and peas can be stored for relatively long periods of time without deterioration. They must be kept dry and cool during storage, and only products having less than 10% moisture should be stored. Brown long-grain rice is not as stable as white polished rice and cannot be kept in storage for any length of time since rancidity is likely to occur. Insect infestation can be virtually eliminated by using the method described in Section XIII. An air-tight container is recommended for best keeping.

Introduction to TVP—the meat that never moved a muscle

TVP has been used commercially for several years by food processors and institutions, such as hospitals, orphanages, and schools. However, it has not been readily available to housewives except in the form of imitation bacon bits. Many flavors are now available.

TVP is a meat substitute made from soybeans and should be stored a maximum of five (5) years when purchased in sealed cans. Bulk purchases in boxes or paper sacks should immediately be placed in cans (to protect it from the light) and stored in temperatures BELOW 84°. Bulk TVP has a lesser storage life and should be used regularly in meal planning and replaced as it is used. It is designed to be used with other meats or by itself. Briefly, here's how it is made: The hulls are removed from the soy bean, then the oil, and what's left is ground into flour. The flour is then put through a giant machine called an extruder where great heat and pressure force the flour out of the machine through various sized holes, much like your home food grinder. This causes the molecules to change, forming chains. This is what gives the product its fibrous, meat-like appearance.

Here are some helpful hints for using TVP:

1. To hydrate TVP use equal parts liquid with equal parts TVP.

2. The liquid used can be water, consomme, bouillion, etc.

3. The temperature of the liquid should be hot, either hot tap water or boiling. This causes the TVP to hydrate immediately.

4. When hydrating TVP chunks, bring liquid to a boil, add chunks, cover with lid, remove from heat and let stand 10-15 minutes.

5. The amount of TVP added to a pound of ground meat depends on you. However, a good rule to follow is 1/2 - 2/3 cup TVP to 1 pound ground meat. **This is a dry measure.**

6. There are a number of ways to add the TVP to the ground meat, and by process of trial and error this is the preferred method:

Method:

Hydrate the TVP (minced dehydrated onion can be added to the TVP at this time to give additional flavor). Mix into the ground meat as you would a meatloaf. This makes the meat and TVP stick together. As the gound meat cooks, the TVP picks up the flavor from the fat in the ground meat. When the meat is almost brown, we suggest you tilt the pan so the excess fat will drain off. The TVP absorbs some of the fat, which adds to its flavor, but too much fat, we feel, ruins the taste of the food.

7. Remember the unflavored TVP will pick up any kind of flavor, so mix it with everything: ground beef, bulk sausage, ground turkey, ground veal, tuna (2 - 4 cup or more to a 7 oz. can), etc.

8. Use as a filler in soups. Throw in a handful dry and it will pick up the flavor of the soup.

9. Can be substituted for nuts in some candies, cookies, etc.

10. Tremendous for snacks...flavored is best, especially bacon bits. Place some in a bowl and watch it disappear.

11. Delicious as an extremely high protein cereal (52% protein). Just add honey and milk to the unflavored and it is ready to eat. Grind fine and add to cracked wheat, cream of wheat or Roman Meal.

12. Use a little more seasoning than usual. Tomatoes, onion and spices enhance its appearance and taste very well. Also serve with gravies and sauces.

13. Sausage flavored can be used in many ways (use pork with sausage spices, available as a mix from some meat markets). Hydrate it and use it on pizza, or try it in scrambled eggs, or omelets. Use along with unflavored to add that special pork flavor to meat loaf, lasagna, meatballs. Anytime a recipe calls for pork or sausage, we add a small amount of TVP. Let your imagination have fun and you'll be surprised at what you can come up with.

14. Bacon (usually used dry) can be used on pizza, in eggs, as garnish on baked potatoes, salads, etc. It is also good in chip dip.

15. Flavor of TVP disappears if it is overcooked. When using it straight without any other meat and,

whenever possible, add toward the end of the cooking time to retain flavor.

Dried Milk (nonfat)

Officially, nonfat dry milk solids are made by removing virtually all butter-fat and water from fresh whole milk. The remaining portion is a nonfat or skim milk powder which contains all of the important nutrients of fresh whole milk except vitamins A and D and, of course, butter-fat.

Non-instant brands take a bit longer to reconstitute into liquid milk and are less expensive than the instant brands. If you use dry milk for cooking, it's more economical to use the non-instant types which ordinarily are packaged in bulk; but when you use dry milk for drinking, the instant types would be less bothersome but more expensive. A best way to reconstitute the non-instant type of dry milk is to use an electric kitchen mixer or eggbeater, or shake vigorously in a sealed container until dissolved. One pound (3 level cups) make about five quarts of fluid milk by dissolving the 3 cups of dry milk in 4 quarts of water. Be sure to keep the reconstituted milk under refrigeration.

Nonfat dry milk cannot be successfully fumigated due to its density, and is not easily stored without proper care. It becomes susceptible to flavor and odor changes upon storage, as well as bacterial spoilage, when the moisture content becomes too high, or if subjected to light. Ideally, storage should be in complete darkness below 70 degrees F. and should store almost indefinitely under these conditions. It is recommended that it be repacked in **airtight** cans or bottles immediately after purchase to give it proteciton from picking up harmful moisture. This is one product that **must be kept dry.** The cans or bottles should be dried out in an oven for a few minutes to eliminate any chance of moisture. **Cool before filling with dry milk.** The protein and nutrient of nonfat dry milk will remain stable almost indefinitely under the above stated storage conditions. Even though the milk may go off flavor after long storage, its nutrition is not affected.

Stored nonfat dry milk should be used as part of the regular food supply. Try cooking with it. It is far more economical and it does not affect the taste of most foods. As milk is taken from the reserved supply, it should be replaced with fresh nonfat dry milk. A practice which will keep the milk in continual rotation is one of mixing one part of the reconstituted dry milk solution with one part of fresh whole milk. The resultant drink is very acceptable as well as economical. If you drink reconstitited nonfat milk, you can make it very tasty with additives, such as chocolate syrup and fruit juices. Stored dry milk, once reconstituted, should be used just like fresh milk.

Physicians say that one can live two months without impairment of health on dry milk alone if supplemented with vitamin C.

Dried and Dehydrated Fruits and Vegetables (Purchased from grocery stores)

Like all dehydrated foods, the keeping quality of dried fruit and vegetables is dependent on keeping it dry. Those items will, under proper storage conditions, keep for over 5 years. Dried fruit should be kept in its original package and stored in metal or glass containers. If the fruit is kept in original packages, several kinds of fruit may be stored in one container.

Dehydrated vegetables will keep better if placed in airtight containers using the treatment methods described under **Wheat.** These products should not be kept in storage for long periods; consequently, they should be used as part of the regular food supply and rotated with newly purchased dehydrated vegetables. If your family is not normally eating dehydrated fruits and vegetables in its daily diet, these products should be tried. Dehydrated food will not keep indefinitely and should not be placed in "permanent" storage. However, concentrated and low-moisture foods, purchased in sealed cans, store well for several years if the container is not opened and is kept reasonably cool. We recommend that you try eating low-moisture foods before buying in quantity.

Eggs

Dried eggs will keep for many years at 40 degrees F., but less time at higher temperatures. Fresh eggs may be stored in water glass by placing them in a container with a tight lid. After the eggs (in the shell) are placed in a container, pour the water glass solution (sodium silicate) over the eggs and place the lid on tightly to prevent evaporation. The eggs will keep 9 to 12 months in this preparation if stored in temperatures below 50 degrees F. One quart of sodium silicate (mixed with 9 quarts of water) will do 18 dozen eggs and can be purchased from a drug store.

Unpasteurized dried eggs should be used only in recipes that require oven cooking. Their use is not recommended in egg-milk drinks, mayonnaise, etc. Pasteurized eggs, however, do not need cooking and may be used in uncooked drinks and dishes the same as fresh eggs. In most recipes it is best to reconstitute the dried egg before using. Two tablespoons of firmly packed dried egg powder, with two and one-half (2½) tablespoons of water, equals one large whole egg. One standard measuring cup of firmly packed dried egg powder, with 1¼ cups of water, equals eight large whole eggs. To reconstitute dried egg place the required amount of cool or luke warm water in a deep bowl. Sprinkle the dried egg over the surface; blend until smooth with a fork or rotary beater. Do not prepare more egg than can be used within a day, and keep any unused portion under refrigeration.

Sugar

White and brown granulated sugar properly stored can be kept indefinitely. Sugar will pick up moisture readily and soon becomes unfit for use if left in open containers in a damp place. This product should be stored dry in metal or glass containers.

Honey

Honey can be stored for long periods of time if it is pure. Impure honey usually contains moisture and/or a microscopic organism which will cause a slow fermentation if the honey is stored in unfavorable conditions. If honey becomes hard and turns to crystalline sugar, merely loosen lid and heat it in boiling water until it liquifies.

Cereals, Prepared Breakfast Foods, Macaroni, etc.(See Sec.XIII)

These products should be stored in the same way as powdered milk. They must be kept dry and free from insect infestation. If kept in recommended storage conditions and free from pests, these items will keep two years; however, it is best to keep them in constant rotation.

Salt (Iodized preferred, except for canning).

Several pounds of salt must be included in the storage program. The only precaution in storing this item is that of keeping it clean and dry. It can be stored indefinitely in the original container. Iodized salt which has become discolored with yellow has not been harmed and is still good for seasoning food.

Baking Powder and Soda

These products may be kept in the original containers up to two years, provided they remain cool and dry. These items must not be heated.

Dry Yeast

A three months' supply of dated "instant type" dry yeast, such as Fleischmann's or Red Star, should be kept on hand and used regularly in a rotation plan in home baking. Yeast should be kept cool and dry and must **not** be heated. Canned yeast may be purchased much more economically, however, and will keep six months at room temperature—almost indefinitely if refrigerated or frozen.

A recipe for making "everlasting" yeast is found in Section VII.

C. FROZEN FOODS

The storage life of frozen foods will depend on how well the food is packaged and the quality of the food at the time of packaging. Well-packaged food can often be kept one or two years in a frozen condition, but it must be remembered that power failure usually accompanies widespread destruction. Power failure of 24 to 36 hours may render most frozen foods unfit for human consumption.

Improper storage lowers the quality of all frozen foods. For example, there is no assurance that the frozen liquids you buy are in good condition. For a test, shake the can to determine that it is solidly frozen; if the contents slosh about, reject the can.

The maximum storage period for frozen foods is contained in the manuals which accompanied the purchase of your home freezer. If you have lost this manual, we urge you to obtain another, as there are a number of foods that will not keep more than a few months.

D. OTHER ITEMS

Water

Canned water, obtained from commercial sources, might also be stored in sufficient quantities to meet the family needs for one or two days. As surprising as it may seem, water is one of the most difficult products to preserve. Home canning of water is not recommended for drinking purposes, as the water is usually not palatable; however, if you plan to store tap water, make sure it's clean and sterile before you store it. Clean the empty bottles with hot, soapy water and rinse well. Fill bottles with clean water to within one inch of the top, put lids on and process as follows:

1. Place bottles in a boiling water bath, boiling quart jars for 20 minutes, two-quart jars for 25 minutes, and gallon jars for 30 minutes

OR...

2. After filling the bottles, use a medicine dropper and put two drops of Clorox or Purex per quart in each bottle. Then seal the lids tightly and store in a cool, dark place.

NOTE: Plastic Clorex or Purex bottles are ideal for storing water. **But,** be sure to rinse out all remaining liquid bleach before filling with water to avoid the possibility of illness from drinking too much bleach.

Do not put home-canned water in metal containers.

In case of emergency, water in your toilet tank (not bowl) and your hot water tank can be used. There is sufficient water in these two sources to last a family several days. If water from rivers or ponds is used, it should be boiled for two minutes or longer before drinking. In the event of an atomic bomb, water should be declared free from radioactive fallout before boiling and drinking.

Don't let empty fruit bottles stand around. They should have either food or water in them. As bottled foods are used, reclean each bottle and fill with water. It is well to keep on hand a supply of glass jars with appropriate lids so they can be used either for storing food or water.

If water tastes flat after opening, it probably lacks air. To aerate, simply pour the water from one container to another three or four times and then refrigerate or cool with ice before drinking.

SEC. VI

FOOD DEHYDRATING
IN THE HOME

SECTION VI

FOOD DEHYDRATING IN THE HOME

An Ancient Art Yields Modern Benefits

—By Jay P. and Shirley S. Bills

If you are interested in giving your taste buds a treat and your stomach a healthful treatment, food dehydrating is for you! Modern techniques are yielding many new and exciting benefits from the ancient art of food preservation by dehydrating...and you never need to worry about freezer or electrical failure when foods are dehydrated.

When the water content of foods is reduced to 10% or less, the spoilage micro-organisms and enzymes are primarily inactivated and, thereby, foods may be preserved almost indefinitely. Dehydrating foods does affect the color and the flavor somewhat, but the nutritional values are present for long periods of time.

Many national and church leaders have emphasized a storage program for many years; therefore, it is vital to not only have food in storage, but to have it in a form which would appeal to the whole family, as well as to know its proper utilization. The information presented in the following paragraphs depicts the current findings on this particular method of food storage and usage...a concise presentation as observed from on-going research...under seven basic topics:

1. Selection of foods to be dehydrated:

Most fruits, vegetables, and some meats, will dehydrate successfully. However, some items, such as citrus products, do not dehydrate well. Not everyone likes the same dehydrated foods, so what to dehydrate becomes a matter of individual preference. The raw product should be of good quality and fully mature **but still firm**. Remove any blemish or imperfection. To peel or not to peel depends on personal taste. Naturally, an item such as a banana, really ought to be peeled!

2. Slicing

Our experience has shown that the ideal thickness is approximately 3/16" thick. Many people tend to use larger pieces, such as peach halves, and then are very disappointed because the time required to dehydrate is very long and/or the fruit spoils before it is fully dehydrated. Using a thin stainless steel blade minimizes bruising and discoloration.

3. Treatment:

This is the only step where there is a difference between fruits and vegetables.

Vegetables: Most vegetables must be steam-blanched before dehydrating to destroy the enzyme which causes the product to continue to mature. This is accomplished by suspending the sliced vegetable over boiling water in a container which will permit the steam to move up through the individual slices. This can be done by using a steamer, a colander, a french-fry basket, etc. The time required depends on the vegetables and varies from 2 minutes (celery) to 40 minutes. (Red beets must be fully cooked before slicing and dehydrating).

Fruits: The treatment for fruit depends on the fruit and the method that will be used to dehydrate the fruit. For example, if the fruit is to be dehydrated in the sun which may take many days, it must be treated to protect it from oxidation until it is completely dehydrated. This can be accomplished by treating the fruit with sulphur **fumes** or slipping it in a sodium bisulfite and water solution for two minutes and draining thoroughly.

Any method which completes the process of dehydrating within 48 hours will not need this type of treatment. However, fruits, such as apples, bananas, etc., which turn dark through exposure to air, should be treated by dipping in a solution of water and ascorbic acid, or Fruit Fresh, or other similar material. The fruit is dipped in the solution for **two** minutes only and removed and drained thoroughly. By slicing small quantities at a time and dipping immediately, less oxidation will take place.

Meats: To date we have experimented in this category with beef and chicken, including making jerky. Jerky can be made using any one of several different recipes, but the main ingredient is raw meat which has been treated with salt or brine to make it safe to eat. If you wish to reconstitute beef or chicken, it must be completely cooked first, sliced ¼" thick, and all fat removed. When the meat is chilled after cooking, the fat is easier to cut out and the meat slices easier. The sliced meat is then dehydrated.

Herbs: These should be selected when mature (but not too old) and thoroughly washed. Do not blanch; simply spead out and dehydrate.

4. Place on Shelves or Trays:

In order to remove the moisture, the food product must be spead out on some type of shelf or food-safe tray that will permit adequate air circulation. This can be accomplished by using cloth netting, screens, trays, etc. It should be emphasized that if the food is piled too deep, air flow will be shut off and spoilage will result. Therefore, we recommend spreading the food product only **one** layer deep until you gain enough experience to know what works efficiently with each product. During the dehydrating process, several vegetables can be put in a dehydrator at the same time, each on a separate tray. The same things apply to fruit; however, don't mix fruit and vegetables within the same load.

We have found that when fruits are dehydrated such as bananas, they tend to stick very tenaciously to the shelves. Through experimentation, we have found that when a strong washable nylon netting is placed on the shelves or trays first and the sliced fruit spread on it and then dehydrated, the fruit still sticks to a degree, but it is much easier to remove. The nylon netting found in most yard-goods stores is not heavy enough and will tear easily.

5. Dehydrating:

A number of methods have been used successfully for dehydrating. Each one has its own advantages and disadvantages. The important point to remember is: If you want a high-quality product, the moisture must be removed as **rapidly** and **continuously** as possible without **damaging** or **cooking** the food. In discussions with Dr. D. K. Salunkhe, Professor of Plant Science at Utah State University, we learned that if the temperature exceeds 145°, the loss of vitamins increases very rapidly. Therefore, all our dehydrating has been limited to the 140-145° F. temperature range. According to Dr. Salunkhe, if the above conditions are met, essentially all the nutrients in the dehydrated food will be retained with the exception of the loss of vitamin C.

The actual dehydrating can be accomplished by using a number of different methods, some of which are described below:

Sun Drying: Products are spread on containers that are tilted to receive the full effect of direct sunlight. Sun drying requires considerable care since the product must be protected from insects with screen or netting and must be carried into a shelter when dust blows or rain falls and before the dew starts to accumulate in the evening. If there is not a succession of sunny days, there is danger of spoiling. This method is slow at best because the sun does not cause rapid evaporation of moisture and the dehydration process is interrupted at night.

Before storing, sun-dried products should be placed in a dehydrator or oven for 20-30 minutes. This will complete the drying process.

Oven Drying: The kitchen should be well-ventilated and care must be taken to keep the heat at a low temperature. Set the oven dial at 140-145° F. and preheat the oven. When the product is first placed in the oven, the temperature will drop, but it will soon build up. **Do not** let it rise above 145° F.

When drying in an electric oven, leave the door open two inches. When using a gas oven, the door must be propped eight inches. This not only helps control temperature, but is essential for the escape of moisture.

The disadvantages of oven drying are many; it is difficult to get sufficient air movement, and most ovens do not control at a low enough temperature to preserve nutrients and color, nor do they have enough shelves to dry a large amount at one time. The product must be stirred frequently because there is no fan to promote air flow.

Home-Built Dehydrator: This can be constructed from a wooden or metal box or an old refrigerator by adding a fan, a heating element, a thermostat, shelf supports, etc. Extensive experimenting must be done to get the right air movement and temperature to produce the optimum drying conditions.

Commercially-bought Dehydrator: Several dehydrators are now appearing on the market and the results vary according to each dehydrator. If you consider one of these, you should look for one which has a heating element to permit dehydrating year-round, a thermostat to control the temperature, a fan to provide adequate air circulation, and a means to pull in dry air and expel moist air.

The amount of time required for dehydrating will vary from 4-6 hours, for some items in a commercial unit, up to two or three weeks for sun-drying of certain fruits, depending on weather conditions. Therefore, it becomes necessary to be able to determine when the food is dry enough for storage purposes.

Before testing to determine if the product is dry enough for storage, a piece must be removed from the drying apparatus and cooled. Vegetables will be hard and brittle. Fruit will be pliable and leathery; if the fruit cracks, the drying time was too long. Jerky will be stringy and leathery; meat that has been cooked first will feel crisp. Learn to determine by the "feel" whether or not the product is sufficiently dry. How dry the product should be is, in part, determined by how long you intend to store it. If you are going to use fruit for snacks in the next six months, it does not need to be as dry as fruit you wish to store for several years.

6. Storage:

One of the big advantages of dehydrated food is the small storage space required. For example, ten pounds of fresh carrots become only one pound when dehydrated. One-half bushel of apples after dehydrating can be put into a gallon jar. Perhaps the most astounding reduction in size occurs when celery is dehydrated; 25 pounds of fresh celery reduces to one pound. However, when dehydrated food is reconstituted, it regains its full size.

If you wish to keep dehydrated food for a long time with little loss of food value, the following three rules should be followed:

1. **Dry:** Dehydrated food should be kept in air-tight containers or it will absorb moisture and start to spoil. You may use glass mason jars, any size. Large metal cans can be used if the lid is **airtight**; we suggest using large food-grade plastic bags inside the metal cans, placing the food inside and tying the top and putting the metal lid on tight. We are also experimenting with large plastic containers to see how effective they are. You may also use plastic boilable cooking pouches and seal them with a commercially-sold heat-sealer.

2. **Temperature:** The storage temperature should be

60° F. or below, if possible. The food scientists talk about the "Browning Rate", or the rate at which the food discolors or turns brown. This browning rate doubles for each 12-15° rise in temperature.

3.   **Darkness:** This is desirable and easily accomplished if your storage room is not completely dark. Jars of food may be wrapped in brown paper, newspaper or black plastic, and the store-room window can be covered with layers of paper, cardboard or black plastic.

Dehydrated food will last two to three times as long if you will put a small desiccant package (a chemical that absorbs moisture) in the container with the food. This will absorb any extra moisture and will prevent spoilage. Examine the food occasionally, particularly at the beginning of storage. If there is any sign of moisture, put the food back into the drying apparatus and dehydrate until all evidence of mositure is gone.

We do not have a good indication yet as to how long dehydrated meat will store, although we have some that is now a year old and is in excellent condition.

7. Using Dehydrated Food:

Experience over the past two years has indicated that dehydrated food can be used in two different ways. Much of our dehydrated fruit is not reconstitited but is· used as 'snack' food. Children thoroughly enjoy this fruit and will eat all you will let them have!

Learning to cook with dehydrated food was perhaps the most difficult step in the entire process. Reconstituting is the method by which water is put back into the food that was taken out during the dehydrating process. Vegetables can be reconstituted in either hot or cold water. Depending on how they are to be used. Most vegetables can be reconstituted and cooked in approximately one hour. Carrots placed in cold water will reconstitute in five or six hours. However, salt must **not** be added to vegetables until **after** they are reconstitited. Dehydrated swiss chard or other greens can be placed in boiling water for 5-10 minutes and then seasoned. This provides a means of having fresh greens year-round.

We are delighted with the vegetable soup mix we have developed and always enjoy watching peoples' reaction when they see and taste the reconstituted soup.

We have found that it requires approximately two cups of water for each cup of dehydrated food. This will yield four to five individual servings.

If you desire to reconstitute fruit, such as in making desserts, the method is very similar to that used for vegetables. Place dehydrated fruit in hot or cold water and soak until reconstituted, and THEN add sugar and use in recipes calling for fresh fruit; or you may cook the fruit as desired.

Dehydrated meat can be added to soups, stews, etc., because it was cooked before it was dehydrated. By the time the vegetables are cooked, the meat will be completely reconstituted.

Dehydrated herbs and celery leaves can be added to any food for seasoning as the food is cooking.

We would like to share some of the new food experiences which have come to our attention. Cucumbers can be peeled, sliced, dehydrated until brittle, and placed in a blender to make a powder. During the winter this powder can be added in very small quantities to salad dressing to provide the cucumber flavoring. We have also blended dehydrated onions and put the powder into a salt shaker for table use. Most vegetables can be dehydrated, powdered, and used for seasoning or made into delicious purees, soups, baby food, etc.

Perhaps the most delicious dehydrated product, as far as we are concerned, is raisins made from dehydrating green seedless grapes that are cut in half. Dehydrating bing cherries make delicious dark raisins.

There are several other big plusses in the use of dehydrating food. In discussions with a physician who is an authority as well as an enthusiast, and who also dehydrates food for his own consumption, we were told that the body can assimilate dehydrated foods more easily than foods which have been bottled in a sugar syrup. Dehydrated foods can add a greater and more interesting variety to a diabetic diet under a doctor's direction, whereas many foods canned in sugar solution are not so recommended.

In discussing food storage with many people, the almost universal response has been that they have stored some food but put it on the shelf and have not used it. This is because the types of food stored is not the type they normally eat and does not permit a wide variety in the diet. However, our experience proves that dehydrated foods can add a great variety and creativity to your diet.

May we challenge you to try it......you'll like it!

MOUNTAIN VALLEY DEHYDRATOR

For Home Drying of Fruits, Vegetables, Meats, and Herbs

For more information, write to:
P.O. Box 692, Logan, Utah 84321

SEC. VII

ROTATE YOUR
PERISHABLES

SECTION VII

ROTATE YOUR PERISHABLES

Here again is **Rule 3.** You cannot keep a year's supply **on hand,** nor successfully store canned or bottled foods without spoilage, unless you faithfully follow a rotation plan.

A number of methods may be used for rotation of foods. Two very successful methods will be explained. Perishable foods must be stored in a location that will provide easy access to them, both in removing older stock and replenishing with new stock. You cannot easily do this if you keep your food in the carton box or case in which it was purchased.

METHOD 1.

1. A good system is to build some shelves of 1" x 12" lumber, spacing the shelves wide enough apart to stack two #2½ size cans with an inch or two to spare. The 12" board will hold a surprising amount of cans.

2. Purchase a grease pencil and mark each article or can with the date of purchase, showing the month and year, e.g., 2/8 for February 1968.

3. Divide your storage shelves into allotted space for each type of food, allowing one extra row for rotation **for each variety.**

For example, you can put six #2½-size cans in a row on a 12" board, stacked two high and three deep. Thus, if you were storing 24 cans of tomatoes, you would have four rows with six cans in a row. Leave the fifth row empty. The storage shelf would then look like this: (showing top view of cans stacked 2 high)

Row: A B C D E

```
   ⌇   0 0 0 0   ⌇
   ⌇   0 0 0 0   ⌇   12" Board
   ⌇   0 0 0 0   ⌇
```

4. Store the oldest dates in row A, next oldest in row B, etc. The new replacement purchases will be put in the empty row E, explained next.

5. You are now ready to rotate. Since row A contains the oldest stock, you first remove for use from row A. For each and every can removed, purchase another as soon as possible and stack in row E, after dating each can with the date of month and year. By doing this you will have row E filled at the time you have emptied row A. You then begin using out of row B, putting newly purchased stock in row A. This way you will always have one row being emptied while you are filling another, hence maintaining your storage up-to-date, complete, on "ON HAND for at least a year ahead."

METHOD 2.

1. This is a slanting-shelf plan to allow cans to roll to the low end of the shelf. Replacement purchases will be put in at the high end of the shelf, thus allowing the oldest stock to be removed from the low end.

2. Each article should be marked with date of purchase as indicated in Method 1.

3. Slanting shelves can be made any length and height as long as both ends are easily accessible. Construct as follows.

a. Slant the shelf one inch to each linear foot of shelf.

b. Space the ⅜ inch guides carefully the entire length of the shelf so the cans will roll freely without binding.

c. Space between shelves according to size of cans used on each shelf.

d. Vertical supports should be spaced no more than 3 feet apart.

e. List of materials:

#1 shelves 1 x 12

#2 supports 1 x 2

#3 guides 3/8 x 1

#4 ends 3/8 x 1

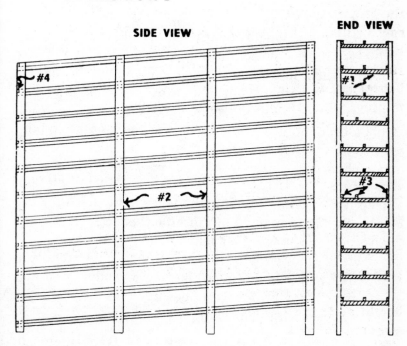

SIDE VIEW   END VIEW

HOW TO ROTATE

If you are following PLAN 1, explained in Section III, and know your family's monthly consumption of rotated foods, here is the best method to follow:

For example, if we were at May 1st, you would refer to your storage list. The quantities indicated under May would then be **physically removed** from the storage shelves.

The foods removed should be placed in your kitchen cupboard or on a separate shelf away from your storage. You will then use these foods during May, because you're using what you're storing. **RULE 1.**

Immediately purchase new stocks of the removed foods and put them in the rotation row, thus maintaining your ON HAND inventory.

By having you physically remove products from the storage shelves in accordance with the monthly list and putting them in a separate location, you will be able to tell soon whether your appetites are changing and whether your list needs revision. When you find certain foods accumulating, merely reduce the monthly quantities on the master list.

Thus, your master list becomes flexible to your appetites. The list will serve you faithfully **only if you keep it accurate.** Therefore, as you see the need for increasing or decreasing any product, change the quantities on your master list immediately.

We'll guarantee you one thing—your family's appetite will change over the years, and a rotation system such as the one explained above is the best way to keep pace with your changing food habits.

NOTE: The author rotates monthly...it takes about 20 minutes.

The greatest concern of people in apartments and small homes is the lack of space for their storage program. This also applies to people who are continually "on the move" such as military personnel. We have two suggestions that have helped many people to solve this problem:

1. Purchase lo-moisture (dehydrated) foods in gallon-size (No. 10) cans because of their ease in handling, longer nutritional life than wet foods, and the need for much less storage space.

2. Locate a blank wall in your home. Build the 12" shelving (Method 1, page 65) from floor to ceiling for your storage items. (Wall standards, brackets, lumber and stain may be purchased from most lumber companies.) Then hang attractive drapes to cover the storage area. Use draw drapes so you can allow air to circulate in the storage area as often as you deem it necessary. The storage area will reduce the size of the room only a foot or so and, with a little decorative ability, could even increase the attractiveness of the room.

SEC. VIII

HOMEMADE PRODUCTS

SECTION VIII

HOMEMADE PRODUCTS

We would urge you to make these products right away, and try them, so you will be prepared and will have gained experience in case you may some day be required to meet an emergency.

Everlasting Yeast

1 quart of warm potato water
½ cake of yeast (or ½ tbls. dry yeast)
1 level teaspoon of salt
2 tablespoons of sugar
2 tablespoons of flour

Stir all ingredients well and put them in a warm place to raise until ready to mix for baking. Leave a small amount of the everlasting yeast for the start of the following time. Keep in cool place until a few hours before ready to use again. Add the same ingredients (except yeast) to the everlasting yeast for the next baking. This way always keeping a bit of everlasting yeast, remaking some each time, will allow you to keep yeast on hand indefinitely.

Hand Soap

1 can of lye
½ cup of ammonia
½ cup of powdered borax
2 ounces of lanolin

4 teaspoons of aromatic oil of rose, lavender, or pine

3 tablespoons of finely ground oatmeal (this is optional

11 cups of melted and strained fat

5 cups of rain or soft water

1/3 cup of sugar

3 ounces of glycerine

Measure the rain water into crock or enamel pan, **never aluminum or tin,** and add to it with vigorous stirring one at a time until dissolved: lye, ammonia, borax, and sugar. Continue stirring until cool. Slowly pour in fat stirring constantly as you pour. Add fragrance and continue stirring for another 15 minutes. While doing so add lanolin, glycerine, and oatmeal. By this time the mixture should be thick and creamy. Pour into molds the size soap bars you want. Enamel or glass baking dish, lined with waxed paper, is good. Let stand until firm. Wrap in wax paper. Let stand a week before using.

Laundry Soap

5 lbs. of grease

½ cup of ammonia

½ cup of powdered borax

1 can of lye

½ cup of coal oil or kerosene

Melt lye in quart of cold water. Dissolve borax in one cup of water and add lye to mixture. Melt grease and add ammonia and coal oil. Add to lye mixture. Stir until congeals. Pour into milk cartons. This soap may be ground or grated to produce granulated, laundry soap. **Never use aluminum or tin container in making soap.**

SEC. IX

WHAT ABOUT
CIVIL DEFENSE?

SECTION IX

WHAT ABOUT CIVIL DEFENSE?

If nuclear bombs were set off at fairly remote distances from where we live, we might very possibly be subjected to the hazard of radioactive fallout. Here are some suggestions for protection if this should happen.

Radio-active fallout is dust and other matter which has been made radio-active by the bomb blast and which has been carried into the atmosphere and is carried down wind from the site where the bomb is detonated. The severity of the fallout from nuclear weapons is difficult to predict. The amount of fallout depends on the size bomb, the elevation from which it was detonated, the type of terrain over which it was dropped, the distance you are from the blast, the prevailing wind, and other meterological conditions.

The fallout is mostly in the form of tiny solid particles. They will settle rather uniformly over a given area. If you are in your house with the various openings closed, the particles themselves probably will not enter the house. However, the gamma radiation from the particles will pass through the walls and windows of your home. It's this gamma radiation that destroys living organisms. The thicker the wall between you and the particles emitting gamma rays, the less radiation you will receive. Basement rooms without outside windows offer the best natural protection in your home. Since fallout is in the form of tiny solid particles, it will not contaminate anything with which it doesn't come in con-

tact. Food in your home will be perfectly safe to eat.
Water from open reservoirs will contain the radio-active
particles, but water from covered reserviors will be
perfectly safe. You can get rid of the fallout particles on
your roof by washing them away with a hose, providing
the radiation level is low enough outside to allow you to
spend a short time outside. If you are outside during a
fallout period, you should take off your clothes and wash
them and the exposed parts of your body as soon as you
reach shelter.

In the event of an emergency your local Civil
Defense organization will keep you informed as to the
radiation level in your area through any of the **local** radio
stations that are broadcasting. If the fallout is too
severe, they may advise you to evacuate. We recommend
that you obtain a battery operated **transistor** radio and
have on hand at least one change of batteries in reserve.
Most of the State Civil Defense Agencies have a large
number of radiation detection instruments which are being placed in the hands of trained people over the entire
state. This will provide Civil Defense with reliable information to pass on to you.

The hazard of radio-active fallout is a temporary
thing. After several days, the radiation level will
probably have decayed to a safe level. It is worthwhile to
consider building yourself a basement in which you can
live for a few days. Three feet of earth will reduce the in-
tensity of radiation to about 1/5,000 of its original value.
A shelter can be constructed quite effectively with sandbags. If you have a basement with windows, it is best to
have sandbags available to cover the windows.

It would be wise to include in our welfare planning a
few other items to help us to meet any emergency which

might come through any disaster. If we have our food and clothing supply on hand, it will place us in a good position from the standpoint of civil defense. One thing we should have however is an emergency kit of items in the basement or the most secluded place in our home. A recommended survival kit is itemized below.

The Civil Defense Corps suggests that the survival kit be kept stocked so that if orders are given to evacuate an area, the people affected can take the kit and have enough food available for a period of two weeks.

List of Desirable Foods for Survival Storage for Family of Four

The kit of suggested foods is given below in amounts large enough to feed a family of four (2 adults and 2 children) for two weeks. If the children are very young, replace some of the canned fruits and vegetables with canned baby foods. Meals can be provided that will satisfy hunger for a fourteen day period—but would not provide for all nutritional requirements for an extended period. It's assumed that pure water will be available. If it is not, the milk can be reconstituted or diluted with fruit juices.

In case of nuclear or other disaster, food in cans will be the safest.

Any juices stored for this emergency will be best if canned with very little salt or sugar. They will have better thirst quenching possibilities if the sugar or salt content is very low.

Choose canned meat which has very little salt for the emergency supply. Much of the canned meat is very salty. Canned roast beef has low salt content. Tuna fish and other meats available in the dietetic pack also contain little salt.

SURVIVAL KIT

Milk
  Powdered, 5 lbs.
  Evaporated, 8 cans
Canned Fruit
  Pears   4 No. 3 cans
  Peaches   4 No. 3 cans
Soups
  Cream soups   24 10½ oz. cans
  Vegetable soups   24 10½ oz. cans
  Consomme   16 10½ oz. cans
  Bouillon cubes   24
Cereals
  Oatmeal, instant 2 pkgs.
  Ready-to-eat   2 pkgs. individuals
Bread
  Bread or biscuits 12 cans
Miscellaneous
  Cookies   4 cans
  Sugar, granul'd 2 lbs.
  Salt   2 small cans
  Hard candy   2 lbs.
  Pickles   2 cans
  Water   112 12 oz. cans

Juices
  Tomato   4 No. 3 cans
  Orange   6 No. 3 cans
  Grapefruit   6 No. 3 cans
Vegetables
  Tomatoes   6 No. 2½ cans
  Peas   8 No. 303 cans
  Corn   6 No. 303 cans
  Green beans   4 No. 2 cans
Canned Meats
  Beef hash   6 16 oz. cans
  Beef Stew   6 16 oz. cans
  Salmon   2 16 oz. cans
  Tuna fish   4 7 oz. cans

  Bakes beans   4 cans
  Spaghetti   2 cans
  Cheese   2 16 oz. jars
  Peanut butter 3 lbs.
  Crackers   tin cans, 4 lbs.
  Gum   24 pkgs.
  Dried fruit   4 lbs.
  Instant cocoa 2 pkgs.

Liquid from canned fruits and vegetables can be used for drinking or diluting milk.

B. List of Storage Items for Emergency Conditions

Cooking Utensils

  4 quart double boiler
  4 quart covered suacepan
  8 or 10 inch covered skiller
  1 large sharp kitchen knife
  1 large cooking spoon
  4 cheap metal forks and spoons

  1 ladle
  1 wide spatual
  1 8 oz. measuring cup
  1 can opener
  1 bottle opener

Paper Supplies

  8 packages paper napkins
  4 packages flat-folded paper
    towels
  4 large boxes cleansing tissues

  1 large stack of old newspapers for
    wrapping farbage, human waste,
    to use as insulating material, etc.
  8 rolls toilet paper

The individual has a choice between paper plates or cheap metal pans with aluminum foil liners. If storage and disposal are no problem, 200 plastic coated paper plates should be on your shelf. However, if use of paper plates is not practical, we recommend purchase of eight cheap pie plates and five rolls of aluminum foil. Foil can be used as plate liners and eliminates dish washing. It also rolls up into small metal balls to facilitate disposal. You should have 200 eight-ounce paper cups or at least six different colored plastic cups. If enough water for rinsing is on hand, plastic is preferred.

Fuel for Cooking

Canned-heat burners usually may be used safely indoors, except in shelters where burning fuel may deplete oxygen supply. Of course, no open flame will be safe when gas, fuel oil, or explosives are nearby. Remember that fire is even more dangerous if the water supply is cut off. To use canned-heat properly, first remove the paper label from around the can. Pry off the cover and touch a lighted match to the can's contents. Never blow out the flame. To extinguish it, slide the cover on upside down. Wait for the can to cool, turn the cover right side up, and press down. Prevent canned-heat from evaporating by keeping the cover on tight when not in use.

Store at least one sterno canned-heat stove and fourteen (14) large cans of sterno (or canned heat or heat tabs) per stove. If the family has a baby, add one can of sterno per day. Store matches in tin box.

Medical Supplies

Band-aids	Adhesive tape 2 in. wide	Vitamin pills
Boric acid	Epxom salts	Vaseline
Bed pan	Gauze pads 3x3	Bandages—elastic 3 and 4 in.
Cotton	Gauze rolls 1 and 2 in.	Desitin ointment and powder
Eye cup	Iodine or equivalent	Milk of magnesia tablets
Ice bag	Kaolin powder (for	Needles and thread
Ice cap	diarrhea and upset stomach)	Safety razor blades
Kleenex	Mentholatum	Sanitary napkins
Lysol	Mineral oil	Sterile applicators
Mustard	Medicine dropper	Talcum powder
Polysporin	Olive Oil	Toothpaste or powder
Scissors	Rubber sheet	Thermometer (fever)
Soap	Safety razor	Water purifier tablets
Soda	Tooth brushes	Invalid or baby supplies
Tweezers	Tourniquet	

Illumination

2	cheap candle holders	2	spare flashlight globes
2	flashlights	1	gas lantern and fuel
6	sets of batteries for each flashlight	24	10-inch candles to fit holders

Miscellaneous

Portable battery radio & fresh battery   Bedding spare clothes, heavy gloves
Hammer, nails, axe, saw, pliers, crow bar, shovel

SEC. X

EMERGENCY SANITATION

SECTION X

EMERGENCY SANITATION

Water

Water is the most important item to consider in emergency sanitation. To insure a safe supply for emergency use, you should store at least seven (7) gallons of water **now** for each member of your family. (See Section V for storage details.) Don't wait until an emergency happens, because it may then be too late to act. Public water service, in case of disaster, is easily interrupted or contaminated. Thousands of people trying to fill water containers at the same time could reduce pressure in the water mains to a point of no supply to your home.

Paper cups and plates are handy items to have if the water supply is cut off, because they need not be washed and can be burned with the rubbish. Paper towels and napkins are good, too, when laundry needs cannot be met. It's wise to store a good supply for emergency use. (See also under **Paper Supplies** in Section IX).

Sewage Disposal

Even if water is available, local authorities may ask you not to use flush toilets, wash basins, and other fixtures connected with soil pipes. The sewer mains may be broken or clogged, which would make it impossible to carry off such wastes. Or water may be needed for fire fighting. It is necessary for every family to know emergency methods of waste disposal. You should know where to find the shutoff valve that controls the water service to your home, and all members of your family should be acquainted with its location.

Failure to properly dispose of human wastes can lead to epidemics of such diseases as typhoid, dysentery, and diarrhea. At the same time, sewage must be disposed of in ways that will prevent contamination of water supplies used for drinking, cooking, bathing, laundering, and other domestic purposes. Here are simple steps that any family can take to prevent such dangers and discomforts:

(a) Your first task is to make some temporary toilet provision, such as portable toilets, for members of your family, especially the children. Almost any covered metal container will do. A small kitchen garbage container with a foot-operated cover can be put to toilet use in emergencies. Anything that has a cover and will hold the contents until you can dispose of them will serve for sanitary purposes at first.

(b) Keep on hand at least one **extra** 20-gallon garbage can or other waterproof container with a tightly fitted cover. This should be lined with paper (preferably waterproof) and the cover should be fastened to the can to prevent its loss. Such a can may be used for emergency storage of body wastes until the public sewerage system can be put back into action. Empty your smaller vessel into it as often as necessary. A small amount of household disinfectant should be added after each use. If you live in an apartment, you may not have a large garbage can or room to keep one. In that case two smaller covered pails or other containers will do just as well.

(c) Keep a shovel on hand if there are unpaved yard areas nearby. Burying human waste matter under 12 to 24 inches of earth is a satisfactory method of emergency disposal. Never deposit wastes, liquid or solid, on the surface of the ground. Insects and rodents may carry diseases to other humans.

(d) Where radioactive fallout does not present a hazard, a temporary pit privy may be constructed in a yard area for use by several families. This offers a good method of waste disposal over extended periods of time. The structure must provide reasonable privacy and shelter.

(e) Persons in city apartments, office buildings, or homes without yards should keep a supply of waterproof containers on hand for emergency waste disposal. Where flush toilets cannot be used and open ground is not available for the construction of privies, such disposable containers offer a practical method of emergency waste collection and disposal. The used containers may be stored in tightly covered garbage cans or other waterproof utensils fitted with lids. Homemade soil bags for this purpose may be prepared very easily by putting one large grocery bag inside another, with a layer of shredded newspaper or other absorbent material between. Apartment dwellers should have sufficient grocery bags on hand now for possible emergencies. A supply of old newspapers will come in handy for other sanitary uses, too, for wrapping garbage, lining containers, insulating bedding from floors, and lining clothes against the cold.

(f) Insecticides and deodorants, such as spray bombs, should be used when necessary to control odors and insect breeding in containers that cannot be emptied immediately. At least 2 quarts of household bleach solution should be kept on hand for disinfecting purposes. Keep on hand also an extra supply of toilet tissue, plus a supply of sanitary napkins.

(g) If you have a baby in your home, it is best to keep an ample supply of disposable diapers on hand for emergency use. If these are not available, emergency diaper needs can be met by lining rubber pants with cleansing tissue, toilet paper, scraps of cloth, or other absorbent materials.

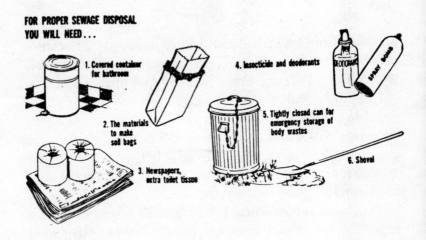

FOR PROPER SEWAGE DISPOSAL
YOU WILL NEED...

1. Covered container for bathroom
2. The materials to make soil bags
3. Newspapers, extra toilet tissue
4. Insecticide and deodorants
5. Tightly closed can for emergency storage of body wastes
6. Shovel

SEC. XI

NUTRITIONAL TABLE

SECTION XI

NUTRITIONAL TABLE

It is important that you maintain essential protein in your diet. At least 2 ounces of animal or 4 ounces of vegetable protein are recommended for each person daily. Following are the main sources of protein:

Item	Oz. of Protein Per. lb.	Item	Oz. of Protein Per. lb.
Most lean meats	3	Canned salmon	3½
American or Swiss Cheese	4½	Skim milk, buttermilk or	
Eggs (fresh)	2	whole milk	1.1 per qt.
Dried beans	3½	Dried milk powder	5.6
Canned string beans	.1	Canned pork and beans	1.1
Canned peas	.6	Dried peas	4
Shelled Almonds	3½	Shelled peanuts	4
		Shelled walnuts	3

The following are considered to be the main sources of food energy in addition to their protein content:

Whole wheat grain or whole wheat flour	2.2	White flour	1.6
		Rice	1.2
Tapioca	—	Dried potatoes	1.2
Fresh potatoes	.4	Dried apple	.2
Fresh apples	.07	Raisins	.3
Fresh grapes	.1	Honey	—
Sugar, granulated	—	Solid fat (animal or vegetable)	—
Butter	—	Dried cabbage	.8
Vegetable oils	—	Dried carrots	.6
Fresh cabbage	.25	Dried corn	1.3
Fresh carrots	.18	Gelatin desserts	1.3
Canned corn	.5		

One ounce of protein equals twenty-eight and one-third grams.

SEC. XII

MEDICAL SUPPLIES

MEDICAL SUPPLIES

TO KEEP ON HAND AT HOME

Remember, the use of any drug should be under the supervision of a physician.

Medical consultants have recommended that only a few simple, effective drugs should be kept in the home—added to only upon suggestion of the family physician to cope with special problems. Here is the recommended list:

U.S.P. Aspirin—regular 5-grain plain. To reduce fever and aches from common colds and headache pain. These do not store well under high humidity or high temperature conditions—perhaps up to 6 months. Replace if the tablets take on a vinegary odor or start to crumble when pressed between the fingers.

Sodium Bicarbonate—plain baking soda. To relieve hyperacidity; also helps to prevent shock from severe burns or injury. Mix ¼ teaspoon of soda and 1 level teaspoon of salt to 1 quart of water and let the victim sip this solution slowly.

U.S.P. Zinc Oxide Paste, or U.S.P. Burow's Solution—To relieve acute skin eruptions or inflamation.

U.S.P. White Petrolatum—petroleum jelly. For chapped skin and a lubricant for an enema tip. Also, may be used for small simple burns.

U.S.P. Laxative—A mild one, such as U.S.P. Milk of Magnesia. Tablets store better than liquid. Laxatives should be on hand only for **occasional** use.

U.S.P. Ipecac Syrup—For emergency treatment of severe croup. In larger doses, to produce vomiting when some poisons are swallowed.

Rubbing Alcohol—isopropyl alcohol 70%. Use as an antiseptic for killing most skin bacteria. Never apply directly on or in a wound. Also used to relieve muscular aches and pains.

Ethical Drugs Prescribed by a Physician—Be sure to have the druggist label the drug with its name and expiration date (the date the drug is no longer fully effective). Throw away all drugs after their expiration date.

SEC. XIII

MEMO LIST
OF STORAGE ITEMS

SECTION XIII

MEMO LIST OF STORAGE ITEMS

The following list of storage items is given merely as a reminder. It is expected that you will develop your own storage list of foods and other items which will suit the requirements of your own family and home.

Products for Rotation—Peanut butter (vacuum packed), dry macaroni, dry spaghetti, dry noodles, milk (canned and powdered nonfat), lids for fruit jars, pectin, vinegar, molasses, jelly and preserves, jello and jello puddings, desserts, cornstarch, syrup, shortening, vegetable oils, canned or bottled; peas, corn, string beans, spaghetti, chili, stew, pork and beans, tomatoes, tomato sauce, yams, tomato juice, cranberries, peaches, pears, crushed pineapple, pineapple halves, applesauce, fruit cocktail, pineapple juice, tamales, tuna fish, salmon, chicken, sea foods, corned beef, beef roast, chipped beef, deviled meats, pork, veal, soups, vegetable juices, vegetable seeds for your garden.

Dehydrated Foods—Hermetically packed fruits and vegetables, stew mix, salad blend, citrus juices, eggs, yeast, gelatin, bouillon cubes, Perma-Pak products.

Permanent Foods—Whole grains, hard wheat, sugar (granulated and powdered), salt (iodized), honey, rice, dried corn and split peas, dried beans.

Household Supplies—Fruit jars and caps, hand soap, laundry soap, clorox, starch, cleansers, waxes, matches, toilet paper, paper napkins and tissues, foil, toothbrushes, tooth picks, shoe polish, clothes pins, brooms, wax paper, candles and holders, needles, pins, thread, light globes, shoe laces, string, rope, light fuses, safety razor, blades, combs, hair cutting set, shampoo, talcum powder, toiletries, clothing and extra bedding.

Medical Supplies—See under **Medical Supplies** in Section IX and Section XII.

SEC. XIV

NOTES ON
FUMIGATION
AND TEMPERATURE

NOTES ON FUMIGATION AND TEMPERATURE

Throughout the world almost half of the stored food supplies are lost due to spoilage, insect infestation, rodents, and mold (mildew) resulting from improper protection from moisture and high temperature.

Reports from the United Nations on foods and agriculture, and our own discussions with dozens of farmers and food specialists, indicate that lack of fumigation and high temperature are the most prominent causes of food losses.

Fumigation—

a. **All** grains (wheat, rice, oats, millet, rye, etc.) should be fumigated in an **airtight** container. Statistics show that the incidence of loss on grain stored without fumigation ranges from 50% for rice to 90% for wheat. In other words, 9 out of 10 people who store wheat for long periods of time without fumigation will eventually lose it to weevil. Some wheat farmers have reported that wheat stored in bins, graineries, or silos have kept well for more than ten years, after which the weevil hatched out and all or most of the wheat was lost. The grain weevil eggs often stay dormant for several years, then hatch out and most grain supplies are lost. Hence, to relieve yourself of this worry, we repeat: **All** grains should be fumigated in an **airtight** container.

b. For other dry products, such as macaroni, spaghetti, beans, split peas etc., we and many others have experienced great success in their preservation by placing one inch of ordinary table salt in the bottom of a container prior to filling and sealing the container. This salt method tends to hold the moisture content down below 10%. Most insects cannot hatch when the atmosphere is less than 10% moisture. However, **do not** use the salt method for the safe protection of grains.

c. Sodium silicate (water glass) is an ideal sealant (to make a container **airtight**) to fill small gaps or openings, such as around lids or fairly tight-fitting covers. After filling the container with the product and the fumigant, tighten the lid and turn the container upside down. Fill the gap around the lid with water glass by using a small paint brush or medicine dropper. **After water glass hardens, it can only be dissolved in boiling water.** Water glass may be obtained from most drug stores.

Temperature—

There are three critical temperatures related to successful storage.

a. 32° —Of course, products that should not be frozen should not be subject to 32° or below. Through careless storage many glass, plastic, and metal containers have broken open due to freezing and the contents lost.

b. 47° —This is the temperature that most insects become active. Ideally, the best all-around storage temperature is 40°. But since practically no person can maintain his storage at 40°, it is absolutely essential that he store properly against insects according to the instructions in this booklet.

c. 84-85° —At approximately these temperatures, fats in foods separate. resulting in rapid rancidity and spoilage. Thus, any food containing fat should not be stored above 84°.

—NOTES—

-NOTES-

-NOTES-

-NOTES-

-NOTES-

-NOTES-

-NOTES-